FRACTION DIVISION

USING LEGO® BRICKS

D1611226

Dr. Shirley Disseler

COMPASS

LEGO® Bricks Make Teaching Fraction Division Easy

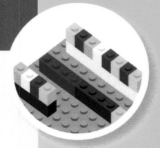

In *Fraction Division Using LEGO® Bricks—Teacher Edition*, Dr. Shirley Disseler has developed activities that work to help students learn how to divide fractions, using a common toy available in most classrooms and homes—LEGO® bricks!

Fractions typically make up the largest percentage of most standardized tests and are one of the most complicated mathematical content areas for elementary school students. Too often, students do not understand why they need to know how to compute with fractions or why certain procedures work. The activities in this book provide clear visual representations of fractions and the operation of multiplication. Students learn the "why" behind the math, not simply the rote procedures for dividing fractions.

In this book, the hands-on activities using LEGO® bricks help students learn how to:
• conceptualize what fraction division means
• divide a fraction by a fraction
• divide a whole number by a fraction
• divide a mixed number by a fraction
• use fraction division in real-world situations

The book starts at the most basic concepts and focuses on a specific topic in each chapter. Most students learn these concepts between grades 4 - 6.

Using LEGO® bricks to model math provides a universal language. Children everywhere recognize this manipulative. It's fun to learn when you're using LEGO® bricks!

Praise for *Brick Math*

"It's hands-on, engaging, and overall, an exciting way to learn. When you bring LEGO® bricks into the classroom, the students automatically react with 'oooh, cool!' and they are hooked on the activity. There is nothing better as a teacher than seeing your students enjoy learning."
—*Tina Lupton, teacher*

ABOUT THE AUTHOR

Dr. Shirley Disseler is Associate Professor at High Point University and Chair of the Department of Elementary and Middle Grades Education, and the STEM Coordinator for the BA to MEd Program. She has over 25 years of educational experience, from elementary school teaching through higher education, including gifted education and exceptional children. Disseler is a LEGO® Education Academy Trainer and serves as the LEGO® Math Expert for Elementary Curriculum Development. She has been instrumental in the development and testing of the LearnToLearn, MoreToMath, and WeDo 2.0 products developed in Billund, Denmark. She serves on the LEGO Education Ambassadors Panel and is the trainer for the High Point University Teacher Academy for LEGO® Education.

Disseler is the author of all the books in the Brick Math series, as well as *Strategies and Activities for Common Core Math, Parts 1 & 2*. She conducts research on engagement and creativity in mathematics classrooms and offers consulting in manipulative mathematics, active learning, classroom management, and learning with LEGO® bricks.

ISBN 9781938406737

9 781938 406737

900

T3-BSZ-808

Fraction Division Using LEGO® Bricks—Teacher Edition

Brigantine Media/Compass Publishing
211 North Avenue
St. Johnsbury, Vermont 05819
Phone: 802-751-8802
Fax: 802-751-8804
E-mail: neil@brigantinemedia.com
Website: www.compasspublishing.org
www.brickmath.com

ORDERING INFORMATION
Quantity sales
Special discounts for schools are available for quantity purchases of physical books and digital downloads. For information, contact Brigantine Media at the address shown above or visit www.brickmath.com

Individual sales
Brigantine Media/Compass Publishing publications are available through most booksellers. They can also be ordered directly from the publisher.
Phone: 802-751-8802 | Fax: 802-751-8804
www.compasspublishing.org
www.brickmath.com
ISBN 978-1-9384067-3-7

CONTENTS

DEDICATION

Dedicated to all those who teach! Teaching requires dedication, patience, and a mind for engaging materials.

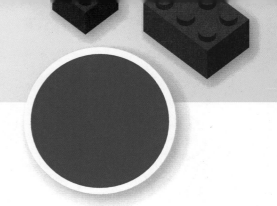

INTRODUCTION

Fractions typically make up the largest percentage of most standardized tests and are one of the most complicated mathematical content areas for young students. Both teachers and parents are often frustrated when working with students who struggle learning fractions. Usually, the problem is that students do not understand why they need to know how to compute with fractions or why certain procedures work. NAEP test results have consistently shown that students have a weak understanding of fraction concepts (Sowder and Wearne, 2006; Wearne and Kouba, 2000). According to research from the National Council of Teachers of Mathematics (Martin, 2007), only 50 percent of American students in grade 8 can identify the correct order of fractions in terms of size or complete math problems where multiplication and division of fractions is utilized.

Jobs have become increasingly more technical over time, which has necessitated that workers be able to use advanced computing skills. Children typically learn basic math skills such as adding, subtracting, multiplying, and dividing in elementary school in first through fourth grades. By grade four, students begin to move into more advanced mathematical content. In most curricula, the first of those advanced areas is fractions. Too often, teachers teach the procedures of fractional computation without explaining the way these steps work or providing visual representations for students. To accommodate variations in learning styles, teachers should use the C-R-A format of Concrete, Representational, and Abstract when approaching math content. Using a manipulative first is key to conceptual understanding and abstract thought. According to research at the National Center for

Sowder, Judith, and Diana Wearne. "What Do We Know about Eighth-Grade Achievement?" *Mathematics Teaching in the Middle School* 11, no. 6 (2006): 285-93.

Wearne, Diana, and Vicky L. Kouba. "Rational Numbers." In *Results from the Seventh Mathematics Assessment of the National Assessment of Educational Progress*, edited by Edward A. Silver and Patricia Ann Kennedy, 163-191. Reston, VA: National Council of Teachers of Mathematics, 2000.

Martin, W. Gary. *The Learning of Mathematics: Sixty-ninth Yearbook.* Reston, VA: National Council of Teachers of Mathematics, 2007.

Siegler, Robert S., Thomas Carpenter, Francis Fennell, David Geary, James Lewis, Yukari Okamoto, Laurie Thompson, and Jonathan Wray. *Developing Effective Fractions Instruction for Kindergarten Through 8th Grade: A Practice Guide (NCEE #2010-4039)*. Washington, DC: National Center for Education Evaluation and Regional Assistance, Institute of Education Sciences, U.S. Department of Education, 2010.

Siegler, Robert S., Clarissa A. Thompson, and Michael Schneider. "An integrated theory of whole number and fraction development." *Cognitive Psychology* 62 (2011): 273-296.

Siegler, Robert S., Greg J. Duncan, Pamela E. Davis-Kean, Kathryn Duckworth, Amy Claessens, Mimi Engel, Maria Ines Susperreguy, and Meichu Chen. "Early predictors of high school mathematics achievement." *Psychological Science* 23, no. 7 (2012): 691-697.

Van De Walle, John A., Karen S. Karp, and Jennifer M. Bay-Williams. *Elementary and Middle School Mathematics: Teaching Developmentally*. Essex, England: Pearson Education, 2015.

Bezuk, Nadine, and Kathleen Cramer. "Teaching About Fractions: What, When, and How?" In *National Council of Teachers of Mathematics 1989 Yearbook: New Directions For Elementary School Mathematics*, edited by P. Trafton, 156-167. Reston, VA: National Council of Teachers of Mathematics, 1989.

Cramer, Kathleen, and Nadine Bezuk. "Multiplication of Fractions: Teaching for Understanding." *The Arithmetic Teacher* 39, no. 3 (1991): 34-37.

Improving the Learning of Fractions from studies of students in the UK and US by Seigler et al. (2010; 2011; 2012), the degree to which a student has fraction knowledge in fifth grade uniquely predicts a student's tenth grade math achievement, above and beyond the student's IQ, family background, or even knowledge of other parts of mathematics. It is clearly worth the effort of providing a more complete way to make sure students truly understand fractions. In fact, research suggests that students should begin learning the basic concepts of fractions as early as grade one (Van de Walle et al., 2015).

Understanding fractions requires that students create a new schema about ordering numbers that is different from the one they learned about whole numbers. For example, children know that 3 is greater than 2 when ordering whole numbers, but with fractions, $\frac{1}{3}$ is less than $\frac{1}{2}$, which can be confusing. According to Bezuk and Cramer (1989; 1991), because of the complexity of fraction concepts, a greater amount of time should be devoted in the teaching process to developing students' understanding of a fraction as a number. But just allocating more time is not sufficient to improve understanding; the emphasis of instruction should also shift from the development of algorithms for performing operations on fractions to the development of a quantitative understanding of fractions through a more "hands-on/minds on" approach.

The real-life application of fractions requires that students have a conceptual understanding of the relationship between division and fractions. Seeing fractional parts as a division problem is helpful. One fraction area where students often struggle is in understanding the meaning of different-sized wholes. Be able to use division with fractional parts gets even more difficult when students lack a clear understanding of the term *whole*.

There are several meanings for fractions that need to be understood by students. These include:

1. Part-Whole Relationships: Grouping the whole into equal parts and taking a portion of that amount. This is the most common use of fractions by teachers and students. (For example: $\frac{1}{4}$ is seen as a rectangle divided into 4 equal parts, where one part is taken.)

2. Fractions as Division: The sharing of some things among a set number of people or groups. (For example: sharing 25 pieces of candy with 5 people to describe $\frac{1}{5}$ of 25 or $\frac{25}{5}$.)

3. Fractions as Measurement: A length, piece, or other measurement part such as area, weight, and volume that cannot be represented with whole numbers. (For example: $\frac{3}{4}$ of a mile.)

4. Fractions as Operator: To enlarge or reduce by a certain quantity. (For example: using a fraction as a rate, such as $\frac{2}{3}$ of a mile in 3 minutes.)

5. Ratio: A fraction as a probability. (For example: $\frac{2}{3}$ as the likelihood of an event happening 2 in 3 times, which can be part-part or part-whole.)

The content in this book is developed to provide students with practice with the concept of different-sized wholes when dividing fractions by whole numbers, dividing fractions by fractions, and dividing mixed numbers. Activities will also investigate the first three meanings for fractions.

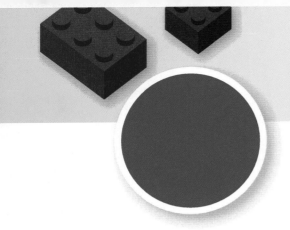

HOW TO TEACH WITH THE BRICK MATH SERIES

Using the Teacher and Student Editions:
Start by taking students through the **Part 1: Show Them How** section of each chapter. Build the models, show them to the students, and ask students questions. Where directed, have students build the same models themselves so they are manipulating the bricks as you are guiding them. A document camera is helpful to display your models to the whole class as you build them. The step-by-step directions in the Teacher Edition work through several problems in Part 1. If you are using the companion Student Edition, have students draw their models and answer the questions in those books as you teach using the Teacher Edition.

Once students have mastered the modeling processes from Part 1, move to the **Part 2: Show What You Know** section of the chapter. Ask students to complete each of the problems using bricks and drawing their models. The companion Student Edition has space for writing answers and baseplate paper for drawing models. Move through the room and check that students are building their models correctly, drawing them clearly, and understanding the concepts being taught.

The Student Edition includes an assessment for each chapter, as well as additional problems for practice and challenge. The answer key for the chapter assessments can be found online on the Brick Math website, at www.brickmathseries.com/assessments. The book also includes an Assessment Chart to track each student's performance on all the skills taught in *Fraction Division*.

Note: Active learning breeds active learners! Students will be motivated and engaged in math when they are using bricks. It will not be silent in your classroom, but it will be full of chatter about the math!

Suggested Bricks:

Brick Math is designed to be used with LEGO® bricks or LEGO® compatible bricks. If you already have bricks in your classroom, your students should be able to use them to make the models. They may have to combine smaller bricks together when the directions call for longer bricks such as 1x10s or 2x12s. Each student also needs a baseplate on which to build brick models.

Each chapter lists the bricks suggested for the lessons in that chapter for every two students, and the appendix includes a total brick inventory that lists all the bricks suggested for the program for every two students.

Specially designed Brick Math brick sets for one or two students are available for purchase from Brigantine Media. Brick sets are packaged in divided boxes and include a baseplate for each student.

Classroom Management Ideas:

- Before starting, have a conversation with the students about using bricks as a learning tool rather than a toy.
- Teach students the language of bricks (baseplate, stud, 1x1, 1x2, etc.).
- Assign brick sets to specific students and always give the same students the same sets. An easy way to do this is to number each brick set and assign the sets to pairs of students by number. When students know that they will always have to work with the same brick set, they are more likely to be careful that the bricks are returned to the set.
- Do not teach using bricks—or any manipulative—every day. Students also need to have opportunities to think through the math processes without having a physical object for modeling. Sometimes it helps to have students draw models without building them with bricks

first. Remember, they won't have access to manipulatives during most tests when they have to show what they have learned.

- To keep bricks clean: Put the bricks in a hosiery bag and wash them on the top rack of the dishwasher. Let them air dry. Clean bricks before assigning sets to new students.
- To keep bricks from sliding off desks, use foam shelf liner cut into rectangular pieces, or large meat trays (you can often get these free from a local supermarket).
- Inventory the sets twice a year and replace bricks as needed. There are a variety of vendors online that sell specific bricks, both new and used. LEGO® retail stores also sell a variety of individual bricks.

SUGGESTED BRICKS

Size	Number
1x1	15-20
1x2	12
1x3	6
1x4	6
1x6	2
1x8	2
1x12	1
2x3	3
2x6	1

Note: Using a baseplate helps keep the bricks in place. One large baseplate is suggested for these activities.

UNDERSTANDING FRACTION DIVISION

Students will learn/discover:
- The meaning of fraction division
- The meaning of the term *reciprocal*
- How fraction division and fraction multiplication are related

Why is this important?

Understanding the relationship between whole-number division and multiplication can lead to better understanding of fraction division because they work in a similar way. If students understand that division and multiplication undo one another when working with whole numbers, they will be better able to grasp the idea that the same properties apply to fractions.

Reciprocals in fraction division provide the link between multiplication and division when dividing two fractions. Many real-world situations involve fraction division, so it is important for students to gain a firm understanding of more than just the mathematical procedures. But students *must* understand whole-number division and its relationships before starting fraction division.

Vocabulary:
- **Dividend:** The number that is being divided into sets (example: in the problem 5 *divided by* $\frac{1}{2}$, 5 is the dividend); usually, the first number in a division problem
- **Divisor:** The number by which another number is divided (in the problem 5 *divided by* $\frac{1}{2}$, $\frac{1}{2}$ is the divisor); usually, the second number in a division problem

- **Quotient:** Answer to a division problem
- **Reciprocal:** One of a pair of numbers that when multiplied together equals 1; dividing 1 by a number gives that number's reciprocal (example: the reciprocal of 2 is $\frac{1}{2}$)
- **Multiplicative Inverse:** The process for obtaining the reciprocal
- **Division:** Separation into parts

How to use the companion student book, *Fraction Division Using LEGO® Bricks–Student Edition*:
- After students build their models, have them draw the models and explain their thinking in the student book. Recording the models on paper after building them with bricks helps reinforce the concepts being taught.
- Discuss the vocabulary for each lesson with students as they work through the student book.
- Use the assessment in the student book to gauge student understanding of the content.

Part 1: Show Them How

Ask students what it means to multiply whole numbers. Discuss how the solution gets larger when you multiply two whole numbers (example: 3 x 4 = 12).

Ask students what it means to divide whole numbers. Discuss how the solution gets smaller when you divide two whole numbers (example: 12 ÷ 4 = 3).

Ask students what they think it means to divide two fractions. Many will answer that the solution will be smaller than the two products. This is a misconception, because students associate multiplying with repeated addition, which increases with each factor iteration, and they associate division with repeated subtraction, which decreases with each iteration.

Show the problem 16 ÷ 8 = 2

Discuss the meaning of this math sentence: How many groups of 8 are there in 16 (*answer*: 2)?

Tell students that this thinking can also work with fractions.

Problem #1: $\frac{1}{2} \div \frac{1}{8}$

1. Discuss the problem as a real-world scenario: Envision a flatbread pizza cut into 8 pieces.

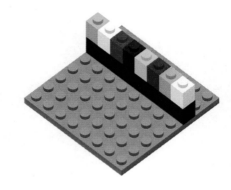

Place a 1x8 brick on a baseplate to represent the pizza. Ask students how many pieces of pizza there are (*answer*: 8). Place eight 1x1 bricks on the top of the 1x8 brick to represent the 8 pieces of pizza.

2. Since the problem calls for only half the pizza, make a model that shows $\frac{1}{2}$ of the pizza. Since 4 is $\frac{1}{2}$ of 8, use a 1x4 brick to show the half-pizza. Move 4 of the 1x1 bricks onto the 1x4 brick to show the pieces in that half. Have students build and draw this model.

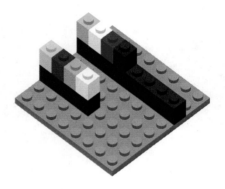

3. Ask students how many pieces are in the half (*answer*: 4 whole pieces). Therefore, the solution to $\frac{1}{2} \div \frac{1}{8}$ is the whole number 4. *Note:* Students should include the quantifier *pieces* when they explain the solution to the pizza problem.

4. Explain how this relates to the reciprocal by referring to the whole number problem, $16 \div 8 = 2$. Use multiplication to see how that answer is correct by using the reverse: $2 \times 8 = 16$.

Students should know that $16 \div 8$ is the same as $\frac{16}{8}$ when written as a fraction. This fraction means $\frac{16}{1} \times \frac{1}{8} = \frac{16 \times 1}{1 \times 8}$

5. In the fraction problem, the model shows this process:
$\frac{1}{2} \div \frac{1}{8} = 4$ whole pieces

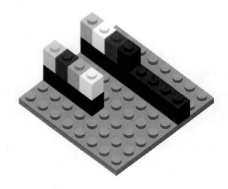

This can be reversed using the commutative property for multiplication as $4 \times \frac{1}{8} = \frac{1}{2}$. If the problem is written like a whole number multiplication problem using the reverse, the fraction is called the *reciprocal*. For example; the reciprocal of 2 is $\frac{1}{2}$ because $\frac{2}{1} \times \frac{1}{2} = 1$ whole.

This would look like: $\frac{4}{1} \times \frac{1}{8} = \frac{4}{8} = \frac{1}{2}$

Looking at the model, 4 sets of $\frac{1}{8}$ (four 1x1 bricks) is the same as $\frac{1}{2}$ in the original model. The model shows 8 studs divided into two parts. Each part has 4 pieces.

6. Rewrite the division problem using the reciprocal of ¹/₈ (which is ⁸/₁) to show the mathematical procedure for solving the problem. ¹/₂ ÷ ¹/₈ = ¹/₂ x ⁸/₁ = ⁸/₂ = 4

Problem #2: ¹/₂ ÷ ¹/₁₂

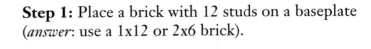

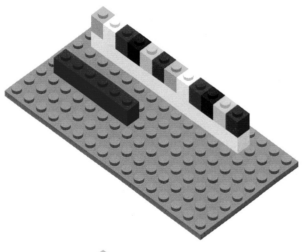

Step 1: Place a brick with 12 studs on a baseplate (*answer*: use a 1x12 or 2x6 brick).

Step 2: Determine what brick is equivalent to ¹/₂ of the 12 studs (*answer*: a 1x6 brick).

Step 3: Discuss the problem as a real-world scenario: If the 1x12 brick represents a carton of eggs, how many eggs are in the carton (*answer*: 12)?

Place twelve 1x1 bricks on top of the 12 studs to show each egg. This shows that there are ¹²/₁₂ in the whole.

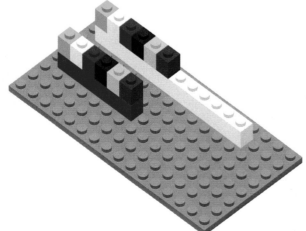

Step 4: Move ¹/₂ of the 1x1 bricks to the model to show ¹/₂ of the carton of eggs.

Step 5: Count the number of 1x1 bricks on the ½ model (*answer*: 6).

Step 6: Write the solution to the problem. Explain the solution.

(*Answer:* ½ of the carton x $\frac{12}{1}$ individual eggs $= \frac{12}{2}$
½ ÷ $\frac{1}{12}$ = 6
A carton of 12 divided into 2 sets = 6 eggs in each set)

This problem shows that the reciprocal of $\frac{1}{12}$, which is $\frac{12}{1}$, when multiplied by ½ is equivalent to 6. Using the multiplicative inverse of $\frac{1}{12}$ makes the math simple.

Problem #3: ⅓ ÷ ⅙

Step 1: Place a brick with 6 studs on a baseplate (a 1x6 or 2x3 brick).

Step 2: Place 6 studs on top of the 1x6 brick to indicate $\frac{6}{6}$ in the whole.

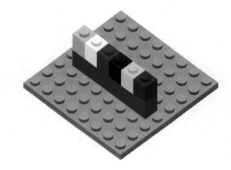

Step 3: Place a brick that is equivalent to ⅓ of the 6 (*answer*: since three 1x2 bricks fit into one 1x6 brick, a 1x2 brick is equivalent to ⅓ of the 6).

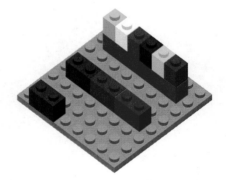

Step 4: Remove two 1x1 bricks from the whole and place them on top of the 1x2 brick to show ⅓ of the whole.

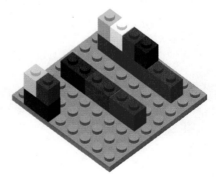

The whole ⁶/₆ = 1 whole

Thirds

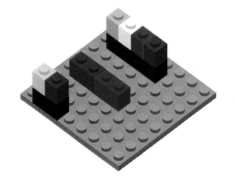

¹/₃ of the ⁶/₆ units
is 2 studs

Step 5: Restate the solution to explain the answer.
$\frac{1}{3} \div \frac{1}{6} = \frac{1}{3} \times \frac{6}{1} = \frac{6}{3} = 2$

Part 2: Show What You Know

1. Can you build a model to solve this problem? $\frac{1}{2} \div \frac{1}{4}$

Step 1: Find the brick to show fourths (*answer*: 1x4 brick).

Step 2: Place four 1x1 bricks on top of the 1x4 brick to show ⁴/₄.

Step 3: Find the brick that is equivalent to ¹/₂ of the ⁴/₄ (*answer*: 1x2 brick).

Step 4: Show the number of studs in ¹/₂ of the ⁴/₄ (*answer*: 2).

Step 5: Draw and explain your solution and label the parts.

2. Can you build a model to solve this problem?
²/₃ ÷ ¹/₁₂

Step 1: Find a brick to show 12ths (*answer*: one 1x12 brick or one 2x6 brick)

Step 2: Place twelve 1x1 bricks on top of the 1x12 brick to show ¹²/₁₂.

Step 3: Find the brick to show thirds of the 12ths (*answer*: three 1x4 bricks).

Step 4: Place 2 of the thirds below the 12ths to show ²/₃.

Step 5: Remove enough 1x1 bricks from the ¹²/₁₂ model to cover the ²/₃ model.

Step 6: Count the number of 1x1 bricks on the ²/₃ model (*answer*: 8).

Step 7: Draw and explain your model solution and label the parts.

Possible Solution:

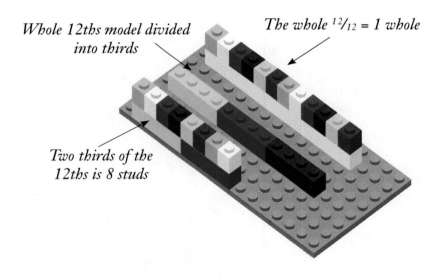

Whole 12ths model divided into thirds

The whole ¹²/₁₂ = 1 whole

Two thirds of the 12ths is 8 studs

$$^{2}/_{3} \div {}^{1}/_{12} = {}^{2}/_{3} \times {}^{12}/_{1} = {}^{24}/_{3} = 8 \text{ studs}$$

3. Can you build a model to solve this problem? $^2/_3 \div {}^1/_9$

Step 1: Find two bricks that when combined total 9 studs (*possible answer*: one 1x8 brick and one 1x1 brick). Use the same color bricks if possible.

Step 2: Place 1x1 bricks on top to show $^9/_9$.

Step 3: Show thirds of this model by finding bricks that make an equivalent thirds model (*answer*: three 1x3 bricks).

Step 4: Place two of the 1x3 bricks below to show $^2/_3$ of the whole.

Step 5: Remove enough 1x1 bricks from the $^9/_9$ whole to cover the $^2/_3$ model (*answer*: 6 bricks).

Step 6: Draw, label, and explain your solution.

Possible solution:

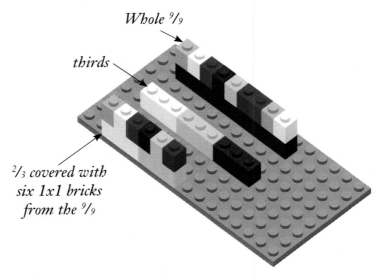

Whole $^9/_9$

thirds

$^2/_3$ covered with six 1x1 bricks from the $^9/_9$

$^2/_3 \div {}^1/_9 = {}^2/_3 \ x \ {}^9/_1 = {}^{18}/_3 = 6 \ studs$

DIVIDING A FRACTION BY A FRACTION

SUGGESTED BRICKS

Size	Number
1x1	15-20
1x2	12
1x3	6
1x4	6
1x6	2
1x8	2
1x12	1
2x3	3
2x6	1

Note: Using a baseplate helps keep the bricks in place. One large baseplate is suggested for these activities.

Students will extend the practice and discovery of:

- Dividing fractions by fractions
- How fraction division and fraction multiplication are related
- The term *reciprocal*

Why is this important?

Division of fractions is a concept that students often find difficult to grasp. More practice will help make sure they have a clear understanding of the meaning of fraction division.

Vocabulary:

- **Dividend:** The number that is being divided into sets (example: in the problem *5 divided by* $\frac{1}{2}$, 5 is the dividend); usually, the first number in a division problem
- **Divisor:** The number by which another number is divided (example: in the problem *5 divided by* $\frac{1}{2}$, $\frac{1}{2}$ is the divisor); usually, the second number in a division problem
- **Quotient:** Answer to a division problem
- **Reciprocal:** One of a pair of numbers that when multiplied together equals 1; dividing 1 by a number gives that number's reciprocal (example: reciprocal of 2 is $\frac{1}{2}$)
- **Multiplicative Inverse:** The process for obtaining the reciprocal
- **Division:** Separation into parts

How to use the companion student book, *Fraction Division Using LEGO® Bricks–Student Edition*:

- After students build their models, have them draw the models and explain their thinking in the student book. Recording the models on paper after building them with bricks helps reinforce the concepts being taught.
- Discuss the vocabulary for each lesson with students as they work through the student book.
- Use the assessment in the student book to gauge student understanding of the content.

Part 1: Show Them How

Review the terms *reciprocal, dividend, divisor,* and *division.* Review the process from chapter 1 with the following problems and discuss the terms throughout.

Problem #1: ¼ ÷ ⅛

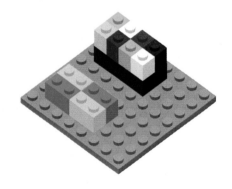

1. Remind students how to model the problem: find a brick with 8 studs to show ⅛ (*possible answer:* one 2x4 brick). Place it on the baseplate and cover it with 1x1 bricks to represent each ⅛ unit of the whole.

2. Place 4 bricks on the baseplate that show an equivalent amount to the whole (*answer:* four 1x2 bricks).

3. Place the number of 1x2 bricks on the baseplate that show ¼ of the whole (*answer:* one 1x2 brick).

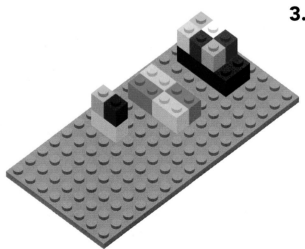

Remove enough 1x1 bricks from the whole to cover the ¼ model (*answer:* 2 studs) and cover the 1x2 brick with those bricks. This represents the solution.

The reciprocal of ⅛ is ⁸/₁. Multiplying the reciprocal, the answer is ¼ x ⁸/₁ = 2 studs.

Problem #2: $^3/_5 \div {}^1/_{10}$

1. Have students place a 1x10 brick on the baseplate as the whole and place ten 1x1 bricks on it to show $^{10}/_{10}$.

2. Find 5 bricks that show an equivalent number of studs to the whole (*answer*: five 1x2 bricks). Place the bricks on the baseplate.

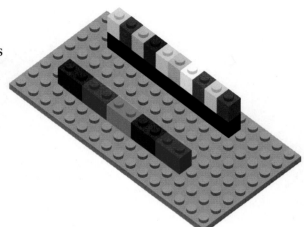

3. Model $^3/_5$ with three 1x2 bricks.

4. Remove enough 1x1 bricks from the whole to cover the $^3/_5$ model (answer: 6 1x1 bricks).

5. Draw and label your model. Explain the solution. Show the procedural solution.

(*Answer*: since three 1x2 bricks show $^3/_5$ of the whole and 6 studs cover those bricks, the answer is 6 studs.

Procedurally:
$^3/_5 \div {}^1/_{10} = {}^3/_5 \text{ x } {}^{10}/_1 = {}^{30}/_5 = 6$ studs

Part 2: Show What You Know

Problem #1: Can you build a model to solve this problem? $\frac{3}{4} \div \frac{1}{12}$

Step 1: Place a brick on the baseplate to show twelfths.

Step 2: Place 1x1 bricks on top of the twelfths model to show $\frac{12}{12}$.

Step 3: Show fourths of this model by placing bricks on the baseplate that make an equivalent fourths model.

Step 4: Place bricks on the baseplate that are equivalent to $\frac{3}{4}$ of the $\frac{12}{12}$.

Step 5: Show the number of studs in $\frac{3}{4}$ of the $\frac{12}{12}$.

Step 6: Draw your model and label the parts. Explain your solution. Show the procedural solution.

Possible solution:

A 1x12 brick shows twelfths. Twelve 1x1 bricks show $\frac{12}{12}$. Four 1x3 bricks show equivalent fourths of 12. Three 1x3 bricks show $\frac{3}{4}$ of $\frac{12}{12}$. Nine studs is the solution.

Procedurally: $\frac{3}{4} \div \frac{1}{12} = \frac{3}{4} \times \frac{12}{1} = \frac{36}{4} = 9$ studs

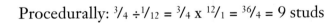

Problem #2: Can you build a model to solve this problem? $\frac{1}{2} \div \frac{1}{6}$

Step 1: Place a brick on the baseplate to show sixths.

Step 2: Place six 1x1 bricks on top of the sixth model to show $\frac{6}{6}$.

Step 3: Place 2 bricks on the baseplate that make equivalent halves of the whole.

Step 4: Place one of the halves on the baseplate to show $\frac{1}{2}$.

Step 5: Cover the number of studs in $\frac{1}{2}$ of the $\frac{12}{12}$ model.

Step 6: Draw your model and label the parts. Explain your solution. Show the procedural solution.

Possible solution:

A 2x3 brick shows sixths. Six 1x1 bricks show $\frac{6}{6}$. Two 1x3 bricks show equivalent halves of 6. One 1x3 brick shows $\frac{1}{2}$ of $\frac{6}{6}$. Three studs is the solution.

Procedurally: $\frac{1}{2} \div \frac{1}{6} = \frac{1}{2} \times \frac{6}{1} = \frac{6}{2} = 3$ studs

Problem #3: Can you build a model to solve this problem? $\frac{1}{3} \div \frac{1}{12}$

Step 1: Place a brick or bricks on a baseplate to show twelfths.

Step 2: Place 1x1 bricks on top to show $\frac{12}{12}$.

Step 3: Show thirds of this model by placing bricks on the baseplate that make an equivalent thirds model.

Step 4: Place one 1x4 brick on the baseplate to show $\frac{1}{3}$ of the whole.

Step 5: Remove enough 1x1 bricks from the whole to cover the $\frac{1}{3}$ model.

Step 6: Draw your model and label the parts. Explain your solution. Show the procedural solution.

Possible solution:

A 1x12 brick shows twelfths. Twelve 1x1 bricks show $\frac{12}{12}$. Three 1x4 bricks show 12 divided into 3 equal groups. One 1x4 brick shows $\frac{1}{3}$ of $\frac{12}{12}$. Four studs is the solution.

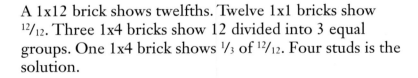

Procedurally: $\frac{1}{3} \div \frac{1}{12} = \frac{1}{3} \times \frac{12}{1} = \frac{12}{3} = 4$ studs

DIVIDING A WHOLE NUMBER BY A FRACTION

Students will learn/discover:
- How to divide a whole number by a fractional part
- That the result of fractional division of a whole number will result in a number larger than the whole number dividend in the problem if the fraction is proper
- The role of multiplicative inverse in the process of dividing a whole number by a fraction

Why is this important?
Students often have the misconception that division means a smaller amount and multiplication means a larger amount. But that concept only applies to whole numbers. Learning to divide whole numbers by fractions helps students clear up this misconception. Dividing a whole number by a proper fraction, such as 4 divided by $\frac{1}{2}$, yields the solution of 8 parts, which is a larger whole number than 4. However, when using an improper fraction (or mixed number), the solution may or may not be a whole number. Students also need to understand the role of multiplicative inverse in the process to understand the concept of the reciprocal.

Vocabulary:
- **Dividend:** The number that is being divided into sets (example: in the problem *5 divided by $\frac{1}{2}$*, 5 is the dividend); usually, the first number in a division problem
- **Divisor:** The number by which another number is divided (example: in the problem *5 divided by $\frac{1}{2}$*, $\frac{1}{2}$ is the

divisor; usually, the second number in a division problem
- **Quotient:** Answer to a division problem
- **Reciprocal:** One of a pair of numbers that when multiplied together equals 1; dividing 1 by a number gives that number's reciprocal (example: reciprocal of 2 is $\frac{1}{2}$)
- **Multiplicative Inverse:** The process for obtaining the reciprocal
- **Division:** Separation into parts

How to use the companion student book, *Fraction Division Using LEGO® Bricks–Student Edition*:
- After students build their models, have them draw the models and explain their thinking in the student book. Recording the models on paper after building them with bricks helps reinforce the concepts being taught.
- Discuss the vocabulary for each lesson with students as they work through the student book.
- Use the assessment in the student book to gauge student understanding of the content.

Part 1: Show Them How

Ask students what it means to divide whole numbers. Discuss how the solution gets smaller when a whole number is divided by a whole number (example: $12 \div 3 = 4$).

Ask students what they think happens when a whole number is divided by a fraction. Many will answer that the solution will be smaller than the whole number. This is a misconception for students because they associate dividing with repeated subtraction, which decreases with each factor iteration.

Problem #1: There are 4 sub sandwiches, each divided into pieces that are $\frac{1}{4}$ of the whole in size. How many pieces are there in all?

1. Ask students to write a math sentence for this problem (*answer*: $4 \div \frac{1}{4} =$ _____).

Ask students what the math sentence means (*answer*: 4 wholes each divided into sets of $\frac{1}{4}$).

2. Show students how to model the math sentence. Since the problem states that there are 4 wholes, use 4 bricks to represent them. But which brick should be used to represent the whole? That is determined by the denominator of the second fraction. Since that number is 4, from the denominator of $\frac{1}{4}$, each whole is modeled by a 4-stud brick (either a 2x2 brick or a 1x4 brick). Have students model the four wholes, draw the model, and label the drawing.

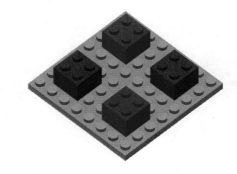

3. Explain to students that to divide the whole number (4) by the fraction ($\frac{1}{4}$) procedurally, you use the reciprocal or multiplicative inverse. Show how this procedure works: use a 1x1 brick to represent $\frac{1}{4}$ of each whole. Have students place four 1x1 bricks on top of each of the 2x2 bricks to show four $\frac{1}{4}$ sets for each of the 4 wholes. Count the number of sets of $\frac{1}{4}$ that cover the 4 bricks (*answer*: 16). This shows that the multiplicative inverse (or reciprocal) of $\frac{1}{4}$ is 4 (number of studs on each of the 4 bricks) and 4 x 4 = 16.

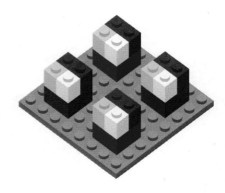

Have students draw the model and label the drawing.

Problem #2: There are 6 pizzas, each divided into pieces that represent $\frac{1}{8}$-sized pieces of the whole. How many $\frac{1}{8}$ pieces are there are in all?

1. Write a math sentence for this problem (*answer*: $6 \div \frac{1}{8}$).

2. Determine which bricks to use to model the math sentence (*answer*: 6 bricks that have 8 studs on each brick—six 2x4 bricks or six 1x8 bricks).

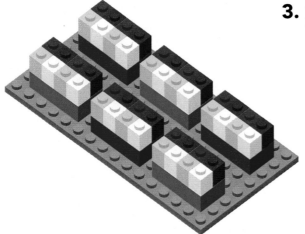

3. Divide each brick into sets of ⅛ by placing eight 1x1 bricks on top of each brick that represents one whole.

4. Count the number of sets of ⅛ to determine how many pieces of pizza there are in all (*answer*: 48).

5. To add to the problem, ask students to determine how many ⅛ pieces each person would get if there were 6 people. Students should understand that each person would get one whole pizza because they would get eight ⅛ pieces. Have students draw the wholes, then draw the parts of each whole to show each set.

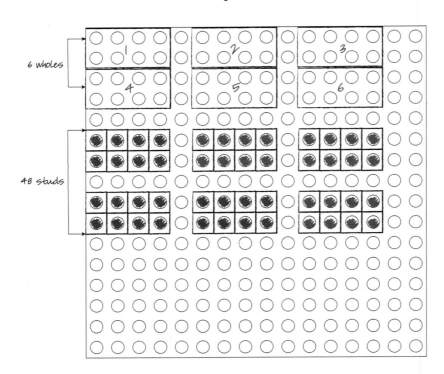

Problem #3: Find a solution for 4 ÷ ²/₃

1. Determine which bricks to use to model the math sentence (*answer*: four 1x3 bricks).

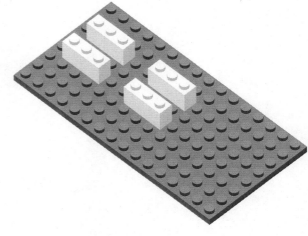

2. Move the 1x3 bricks together and cover them completely with 2-stud bricks. Explain that 2-stud bricks are being used because 2 is the denominator of ³/₂, which is the reciprocal of ²/₃.

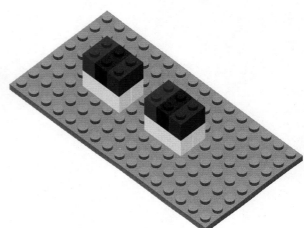

3. Count the number of 1x2 bricks covering the model (*answer*: 6). The solution is 4 ÷ ²/₃ = 6 bricks. Have students draw the wholes, then draw the parts of each whole to show each set.

4 wholes

move together
to make 2 sets

6 (1x2) bricks
to show set
of "2"

Answer = 6 bricks

Part 2: Show What You Know

Problem #1: Can you build a model to show the solution to this problem? 6 ÷ ¹⁄₆

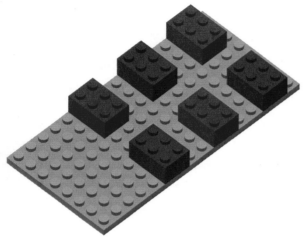

six 2x3 bricks

Step 1: Determine how many bricks and how many studs on each brick are needed to build a model that shows the math sentence (*answer:* 6 bricks with 6 studs on each brick).

Step 2: On the model, show the division of each of the bricks into ¹⁄₆ pieces, using 1x1 bricks.

Step 3: Count the number of ¹⁄₆ pieces in all (*answer:* 36).

Step 4: Draw a model of your steps. Write a statement that explains the multiplicative property for the solution and label it in the drawing.

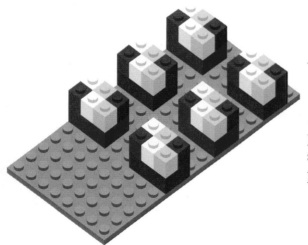

6 wholes divided into 36 ¹⁄₆-sized pieces

Possible solution

⁶⁄₁ is the inverse of ¹⁄₆, therefore, when you use the inverse, you multiply. Since ⁶⁄₁ is the same as 6, multiply 6 x 6 = 36, which gives the number of studs in the solution. This means that 6 wholes divided into ¹⁄₆-sized pieces is equivalent to 36 pieces.

Problem #2: Can you find the quotient? 8 ÷ ¼

Step 1: Determine which bricks are needed to model the math sentence (*answer*: 8 bricks, each with 4 studs).

Step 2: To find the quotient, determine how many ¼ pieces cover the 8 bricks (*answer*: 32).

Step 3: Draw the wholes, then draw the parts of each whole to show each set. Label your drawing.

*eight 2x2
bricks*

Possible solution

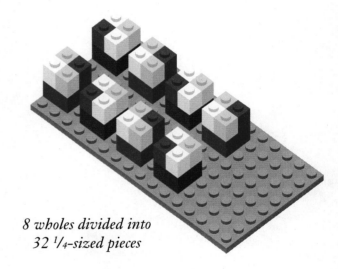

*8 wholes divided into
32 ¼-sized pieces*

Problem #3: Can you find the quotient? $6 \div \frac{2}{3}$

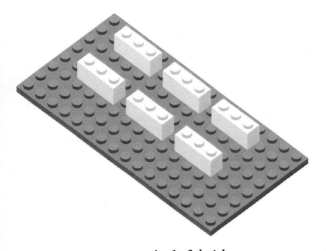

six 1x3 bricks

Step 1: Determine which bricks are needed to model the math sentence (*answer*: 6 bricks, each with 3 studs).

Step 2: Determine which brick will model $\frac{2}{3}$ (*answer*: a 1x2 brick).

Step 3: Pull the bricks together and cover them with 1x2 bricks. Completely cover the model with 1x2 bricks, since 2 is the denominator for the reciprocal of $\frac{2}{3}$, which is $\frac{3}{2}$.

Step 4: To find the quotient, count the number of 1x2 bricks used (*answer*: 9).

Step 5: Draw the wholes, then draw the parts of each whole to show each set. Label your drawing.

Possible solution

6 wholes divided into nine $\frac{2}{3}$-sized pieces

DIVIDING A MIXED NUMBER BY A FRACTION

SUGGESTED BRICKS

Size	Number
1x1	20
1x2	24
1x3	12-15
1x4	8-10
1x6	6
1x8	4
1x10	4
1x12	2
2x2	10
2x3	6
2x4	8
2x6	4
2x8	2

Note: Using a baseplate helps keep the bricks in place. One large baseplate is suggested for these activities.

Students will learn/discover/practice:
- How to divide mixed numbers by fractions
- How to represent division of mixed numbers using a linear model

Why is this important?
In fourth grade, students learn that the addition of three unit fractions, such as $\frac{1}{2} + \frac{1}{2} + \frac{1}{2}$, results in a mixed number, such as $1\frac{1}{2}$ or $\frac{3}{2}$. This lesson expands this idea to division of mixed numbers and includes both whole numbers and fractional parts. This skill is transferable to real-world measurements, distances, and time. Understanding parts of the whole is key, and using a model helps students understand conceptually where the parts come from in the procedural calculation.

Vocabulary:
- **Dividend:** The number that is being divided into sets (example: in the problem *5 divided by* $\frac{1}{2}$, 5 is the dividend); usually, the first number in a division problem
- **Divisor:** The number by which another number is divided (in the problem *5 divided by* $\frac{1}{2}$, $\frac{1}{2}$ is the divisor); usually, the second number in a division problem
- **Quotient:** Answer to a division problem

- **Reciprocal:** One of a pair of numbers that when multiplied together equals 1; dividing 1 by a number gives that number's reciprocal (example: reciprocal of 2 is $\frac{1}{2}$)
- **Multiplicative Inverse:** The process for obtaining the reciprocal
- **Division:** Separation into parts
- **Mixed Number:** A number consisting of a whole number and a fraction or decimal part (examples: $2\frac{1}{2}$ or 2.5)

How to use the companion student book, *Fraction Division Using LEGO® Bricks–Student Edition*:

- After students build their models, have them draw the models and explain their thinking in the student book. Recording the models on paper after building them with bricks helps reinforce the concepts being taught.
- Discuss the vocabulary for each lesson with students as they work through the student book.
- Use the assessment in the student book to gauge student understanding of the content.

Part 1: Show Them How

Remind students what it means to divide fractions and review the processes and vocabulary from earlier chapters:

Ask students what it means to divide. Students should understand that division means to separate wholes into pieces based a given constraint such as the number of groups. For example, 12 divided by 3 can be written as $\frac{12}{3}$, which means "How many sets of 3 fit into 12?" *Note*: Bricks can be used to prove this concept if necessary.

Ask students what happens when you divide a whole number such as 2 by a fraction such as $\frac{1}{2}$. Students should understand that the answer is the whole number 4, because the problem is asking how many sets of $\frac{1}{2}$ are in 2 wholes. *Note*: Use bricks to show this. Place two 1x2 bricks on a baseplate, and then cover those bricks with 1x1 bricks. Count the 4 bricks to show the solution.

Explain to students that to divide mixed numbers by fractions, we will put these concepts together with mixed numbers. Ask students: What is a mixed number?

Students should answer that a mixed number is a number consisting of a whole number and fraction or decimal part. Examples: 2½ or 2.5

Problem #1: 2½ ÷ ½
Note: It is important for students to draw their models as they work through each step of the problem.

1. Ask students what the math sentence means (*answer*: how many groups of ½ sets will fit into 2 wholes and ½).

2. To determine which brick to use to model the mixed number, look at the fraction of the mixed number (½). Since the denominator is 2, use a 1x2 brick to represent the whole. Place two 1x2 bricks on a baseplate to show 2 wholes. To represent ½, add one 1x1 brick to the model, since 1 stud is half of the whole of 2. Have students build the model of 2½ and draw it.

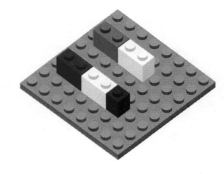

3. Ask students to find a brick that shows ½ of each whole because they are dividing by ½ (*answer*: a 1x1 brick). Have students model 3 wholes using 1x1 bricks that each represent ½. Ask students how many 1x1 bricks are needed to model 3 wholes (*answer*: six 1x1 bricks). Place them below the model of 2½. *Note*: Make sure students understand that the ½ in the mixed number is part of a third whole from which the ½ is taken.

Have students draw this addition to their models.

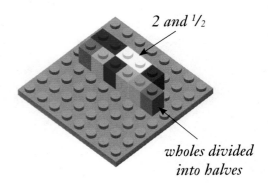

2 and ½

wholes divided into halves

4. Ask students to determine how many sets of ½ are in the 2 wholes (*answer*: 4).

To determine the fractional part of the quotient, look at the bricks that are left in the 2½ model (answer: one 1x1 brick or 1 stud). That 1 stud is ½ of the third whole, which shows that there are 5 sets of ½ in 2½, and the quotient is 5.

Have students label their drawings to show how they arrived at the solution.

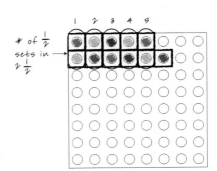

Problem #2: Use a model to find the quotient of 1³/₄ ÷ ¹/₂.

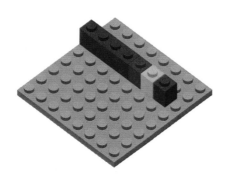

1. Build a model of 1³/₄ using one 1x4 brick to represent the whole (based on the denominator 4) and three 1x1 bricks to represent ³/₄. Have students draw the model.

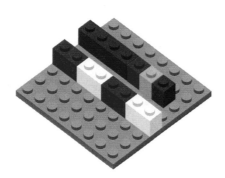

2. Model the division by ¹/₂. Since the divisor is ¹/₂, find the brick that is half of the whole 1x4 brick (*answer*: 1x2 brick). Using the 1x2 bricks, model 2 wholes below the model of 1³/₄ (*answer*: four 1x2 bricks). Have students draw this step.

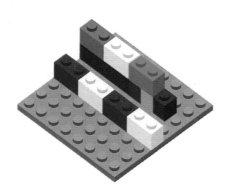

3. Determine how many 1x2 bricks can fit into the model of 1³/₄. Place bricks on top of the model of 1³/₄ (*answer*: three 1x2 bricks fit on the model, with one stud uncovered). Have students draw this step.

4. Cover the one stud that is uncovered with one 1x1 brick, which is ¹/₂ of the 1x2 brick. This models the fractional part of ¹/₂. The quotient is 3¹/₂.

Have students draw this step, and label and explain the drawings.

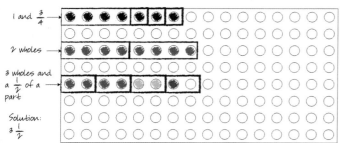

Problem #3: Use a model to find the solution for $2\frac{1}{6} \div \frac{2}{3}$.

1. Since the denominator of $\frac{1}{6}$ is 6, use 1x6 bricks to model the whole number (*answer*: two 1x6 bricks are used to model 2, and one 1x1 brick is used to model $\frac{1}{6}$).

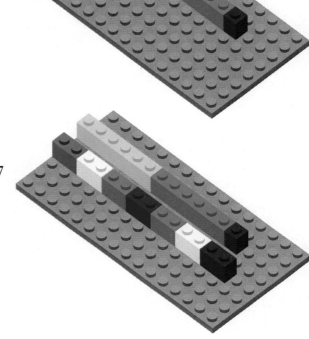

2. Based on the second fraction (the divisor), determine which brick is used to represent $\frac{1}{3}$ of the 1x6 brick (*answer*: a 1x2 brick represents $\frac{1}{3}$ of a 1x6 brick, and 7 of the 1x2 bricks are needed).

3. Three 1x2 bricks model each whole, with each 1x2 brick representing $\frac{1}{3}$ of the whole. Since the divisor in the problem is $\frac{2}{3}$, determine how many $\frac{2}{3}$ sets there are in $2\frac{1}{6}$. This can be modeled by stacking $\frac{2}{3}$ sets on top of the model of $2\frac{1}{6}$ or placing $\frac{2}{3}$ sets next to the model of $2\frac{1}{6}$. *Note*: It can help to better define $\frac{2}{3}$ by using a 1x4 brick to show $\frac{2}{3}$. A 1x4 brick covers two 1x2 bricks, so using this brick to represent $\frac{2}{3}$ shows 3 wholes.

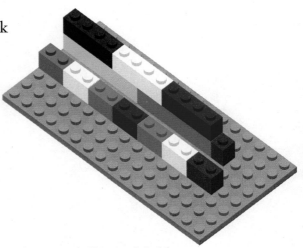

three sets of $\frac{2}{3}$ modeled by
1x4 bricks

4 To determine the fractional part, look at the 1 stud not covered by the 1x4 bricks. Since one stud is ¹/₄ of the 1x4 brick, the fraction is ¹/₄. The solution to the problem is 3¹/₄.

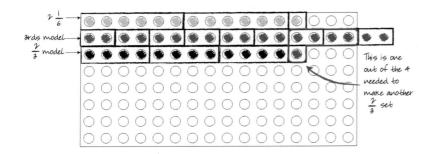

Part 2: Show What You Know

Problem #1: Can you find the solution to this problem using a model? 4¹/₂ ÷ ¹/₂

Step 1: Determine the bricks to model 4 and ¹/₂ (*answer*: four 1x2 bricks to model 4 and one 1x1 brick to model ¹/₂).

Step 2: Find the brick that divides the whole into halves and place enough of them on the baseplate to show the whole number (*answer*: ten 1x1 bricks).

Step 3: Determine how many ¹/₂ sets fit into 4¹/₂.

Step 4: Draw, label, and explain your solution.

Possible solution

4¹/₂ using four 1x2 bricks and one 1x1 brick

5 divided into halves

Nine 1x1 bricks show the solution of 9

Problem #2: Can you find the solution to this problem using a model? 3³/₄ ÷ ¹/₂

Step 1: Determine the bricks to model 3 and ³/₄ (*answer*: three 1x4 bricks and three 1x1 bricks).

Step 2: Find the brick that divides each whole into halves and place enough of them on the baseplate to show the whole number (*answer*: eight 1x2 bricks).

Step 3: Use stacking or counting to determine the number of 1x2 bricks that fit on the model (*answer*: 7 sets of ¹/₂ fit, with one stud not covered).

Step 4: Determine the fractional part of the solution. Think about what one entire set looks like (*answer*: a 1x2 brick) and then how many studs are shown of that brick (*answer*: 1 stud). (*Answer*: the fractional part of the solution is ¹/₂.)

Step 5: Draw, label, and explain your solution.

Possible solution

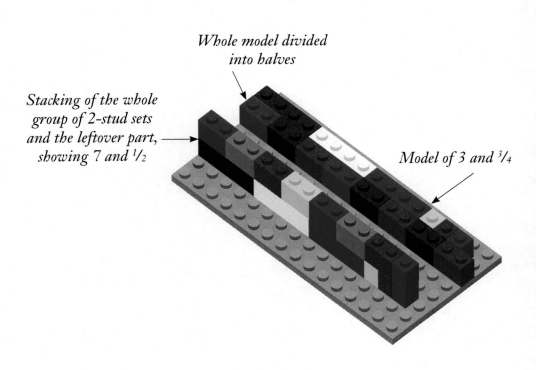

Whole model divided into halves

Stacking of the whole group of 2-stud sets and the leftover part, showing 7 and ¹/₂

Model of 3 and ³/₄

$$3³/₄ ÷ ¹/₂ = 7¹/₂$$

Problem #3: Can you find the solution to this problem using a model? $1\frac{1}{3} \div \frac{2}{3}$

Step 1: Determine the bricks to model $1\frac{1}{3}$ (*answer*: one 1x3 brick and one 1x1 brick).

Step 2: Find the bricks that divide the entire model into thirds (*answer*: three 1x1 bricks, plus one more 1x1 brick) and place them on the baseplate.

Step 3: Find a brick that shows $\frac{2}{3}$ (*answer*: 1x2 brick). Place it below the model of thirds.

Step 4: Show the number of sets of $\frac{2}{3}$ that are in $1\frac{1}{3}$ by stacking or counting (*answer*: 2).

Step 5: Draw, label, and explain your solution.

Possible solution:

2 sets of $\frac{2}{3}$ fit into 1 and $\frac{1}{3}$, so $1\frac{1}{3} \div \frac{2}{3} = 2$

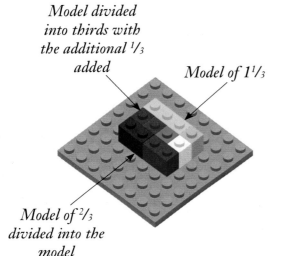

Model divided into thirds with the additional $\frac{1}{3}$ added

Model of $1\frac{1}{3}$

Model of $\frac{2}{3}$ divided into the model

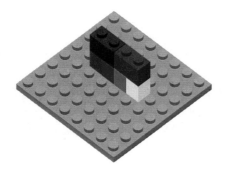

Alternative model using the stacking method

WORD PROBLEMS

SUGGESTED BRICKS

Size	Number
1x1	24
1x2	12
1x3	6
1x4	6
1x10	2
2x10	1

Note: Using a baseplate helps keep the bricks in place. One large baseplate is suggested for these activities.

Students will learn/discover:
* How to use fraction division in everyday life situations

Why is this important?
When students learn how fraction division comes up in everyday life situations, they begin to learn what fraction division actually means. Seeing math integrated into areas such as cooking, traveling, and measurement brings a deeper understanding of the math that students do not learn when fraction division is taught in a strictly procedural manner.

Vocabulary:
* **Dividend:** The number that is being divided into sets (example: in the problem *5 divided by $\frac{1}{2}$*, 5 is the dividend); usually, the first number in a division problem
* **Divisor:** The number by which another number is divided (in the problem *5 divided by $\frac{1}{2}$*, $\frac{1}{2}$ is the divisor); usually, the second number in a division problem
* **Quotient:** Answer to a division problem
* **Reciprocal:** One of a pair of numbers that when multiplied together equals 1; dividing 1 by a number gives that number's reciprocal (example: reciprocal of 2 is $\frac{1}{2}$)
* **Multiplicative Inverse:** The process for obtaining the reciprocal
* **Division:** Separation into parts
* **Mixed Number:** A number consisting of a whole number and a fraction or decimal part (examples: $2\frac{1}{2}$ or 2.5)

How to use the companion student book, *Fraction Division Using LEGO® Bricks–Student Edition*:

- After students build their models, have them draw the models and explain their thinking in the student book. Recording the models on paper after building them with bricks helps reinforce the concepts being taught.
- Discuss the vocabulary for each lesson with students as they work through the student book.
- Use the assessment in the student book to gauge student understanding of the content.

Part 1: Show Them How

Using fraction division in real-world situations is different than just being able to compute with fractions. In this chapter, students apply their understanding of fraction division to real-world scenarios. Students should be able to determine the constraints in the problem. Demonstrating how to set up the problem is an important step in the modeling process.

Problem #1:

Shelby has been watching a tree grow outside her window and gathering measurements for science class. The tree has grown ½ inch each month and is now 4 inches taller. How many months has Shelby been taking measurements?

1. Help students determine how to set up the problem. Ask students:
   - What is the problem asking? (*answer*: how many sets of ½-inch fit into 4 whole inches)
   - How do you create the wholes for the model? (*answer*: by looking at the denominator of the fraction in the problem, which is ½)
   - Which brick is used to model one whole? (*answer*: 1x2 brick)

2. Model 4 wholes using 1x2 bricks.

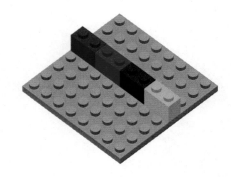

3. Determine what brick represents ½ of the whole (*answer*: 1x1 brick).

Place 1x1 bricks next to the model of 4 wholes. Count the 1x1 bricks to determine how many halves are in 4 wholes. How many 1x1 bricks are in the model? (*answer*: 8 bricks)

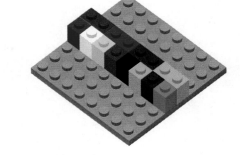

4. Have students write a math sentence that states the problem and the solution (*answer*: 4 ÷ ½ = 8 months). Have students draw their model and explain their thinking.

Problem #2:

Ryan is painting his room. He needs 1½ gallons of paint for all 4 walls. How much of a gallon will he need for each wall if he uses the same amount for each one?

Note: This problem works a bit differently because it is a mixed number.

1. Help students determine how to set up the problem. Ask students:
- What is the problem asking? (*answer*: how much paint will be used on each of 4 walls)
- Think about the computational set-up of the problem. How should the math sentence be written to tell the story? (*answer*: to explain that 1½ gallons is being equally spread across 4 walls, the math sentence is 1½ ÷ 4)

- How do you create the wholes for the model? (*answer*: look at the denominator of the mixed number in the problem, which is 2)
- Which brick is used to model one whole? (*answer*: 1x2 brick)

2. Model 4 wholes with four 1x2 bricks. How many studs are there in the model (*answer*: 8)? This is the denominator of the solution.

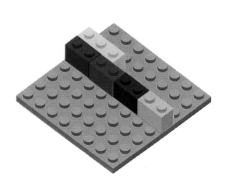

3. Determine what brick to use to represent $1\frac{1}{2}$, to show the total amount of paint. Since one whole is represented by 2 studs, $1\frac{1}{2}$ wholes would be represented by 3 studs (*answer*: a 1x3 brick). Place a 1x3 brick above the four 1x2 bricks. Count the number of studs (*answer*: 3). This brick represents the numerator in the problem.

4. Have students write a math sentence that states the problem and shows the solution (*answer*: $1\frac{1}{2} \div 4 = \frac{3}{8}$ of a gallon per wall). Have students draw their model and explain their thinking.

Problem #3:

Toby is running a lemonade stand to raise money for charity. This morning, he has 6 quarts of lemonade, and a stack of big paper cups that each hold $\frac{1}{3}$ of a quart. How many servings of lemonade can he sell?

1. Help students determine how to set up the problem. Ask students:
- What is the problem asking? (*answer*: how many servings will 6 quarts of lemonade fill?
- Think about the computational set-up of the problem. How should it be written to tell the story? (*answer*: 6 quarts is being divided into sets of $\frac{1}{3}$, so the math sentence is $6 \div \frac{1}{3}$).

- How do you create the wholes for the model? (*answer*: look at the denominator of the fraction in the problem, which is 3)
- Which brick is used to model one whole? (*answer*: a 1x3 brick)

2. Model 6 wholes with six 1x3 bricks. Count the studs (*answer*: 18). *Note*: students can work with a partner and put their baseplates together if necessary.

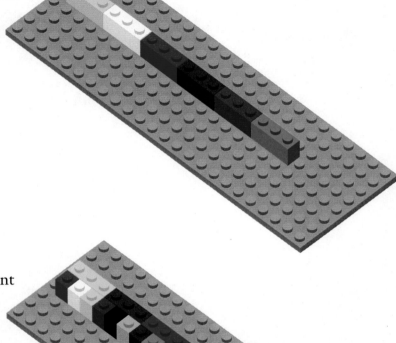

3. Determine what brick to use to represent ⅓ (*answer*: a 1x1 brick). Place 1x1 bricks below the 1x3 bricks to show how many glasses of lemonade can be poured from the 6 quarts (*answer*: 18).

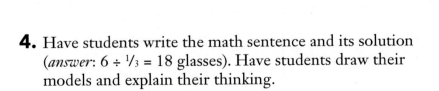

4. Have students write the math sentence and its solution (*answer*: 6 ÷ ⅓ = 18 glasses). Have students draw their models and explain their thinking.

Part 2: Show What You Know

Problem #1:

Jamie is making yogurt and putting it into ½-cup containers. If she makes ¾ of a gallon of yogurt, how many containers does she need? (*Hint*: 16 cups in one gallon)

Possible solution:

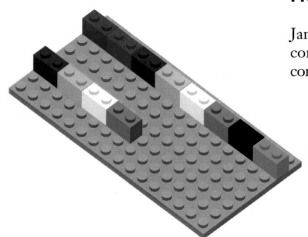

Students should first use the hint to determine that ¾ of a gallon is 12 cups and that each whole cup is modeled with a 1x2 brick (based on the denominator of ½).

12 cups (¾ gallon) modeled with 12 1x2 bricks

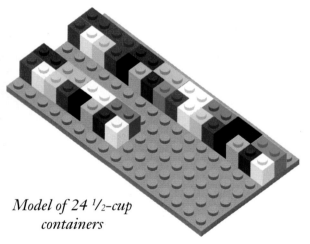

Students should then determine that a 1x1 brick is ½ of the 1x2 brick that represents the whole. They should place the 1x1 bricks below the 1x2 bricks, then count the 1x1 bricks to see that the number of ½-cup containers needed is 24.

Model of 24 ½-cup containers

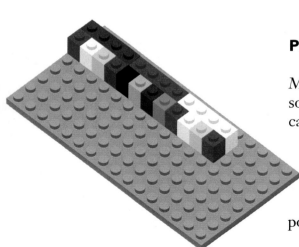

Problem #2:

Mary is planting flowers into pots. She needs ¼ of a bag of soil for each pot. If she has 3 bags of soil, how many pots can she plant?

Possible solution:

The whole is modeled with three 1x4 bricks. There are 12 pots that can be planted with the 3 bags of soil.

Problem #3:

Mark has ¹/₃ of an hour to read and watch TV after school. He wants to split his time equally between the two activities. How much time will he spend on each activity?

Possible solution:

First, determine what ¹/₃ of an hour is equivalent to in minutes. This can be done by multiplying ¹/₃ x 60 or dividing 60 by 3 (answer: ¹/₃ hour = 20 minutes).

Build a model of 20 studs (one 2x10 brick, or any combination of 20 studs).

Since there are 2 activities, divide the 20 studs into 2 sets.

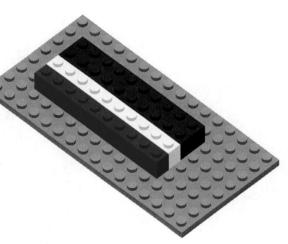

There are 2 sets of 10. This means that if Mark spends ¹/₃ of an hour (or 20 minutes) on 2 activities equally, he will spend 10 minutes on each activity.

Problem #4:

Susan has 3 large bags of candy. She wants to divide it into small bags, each holding ¹/₃ of a large bag. How many small bags does she need?

Possible solution:

The 3 wholes (the large bags) are modeled by three 1x3 bricks because the denominator of the fraction is 3. Dividing this into sets of ¹/₃ with 1x1 bricks shows 9 sets in the 3 wholes. Susan will need 9 small bags.

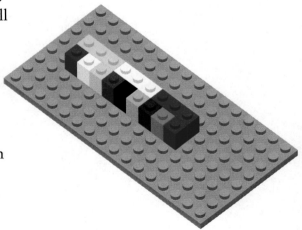

APPENDIX

- **Suggested Brick Inventory**
- **Student Assessment Chart**
- **Baseplate Paper**

SUGGESTED BRICK INVENTORY

SIZE	NUMBER
1x1	84 (32 each of two colors and 10 each of two more colors)
1x2	25 (10 each of two colors and 5 of a third color)
1x3	12 (6 each of two colors)
1x4	10
1x6	10
1x8	6
1x10	6
1x12	5
1x16	2
2x2	12
2x3	6
2x4	9
2x6	4
2x8	2
2x10	2

FRACTION DIVISION
Student Assessment Chart

Name _____

Performance Skill	Not yet	With help	On target	Comments
I can model and explain what it means to divide fractions.				
I can model and explain division of two fractions.				
I can model and explain how to divide a whole number by a fraction.				
I can model and explain how to divide mixed numbers.				
I can apply division of fractions to word problems.				
I can use vocabulary for fraction division appropriately.				

BASEPLATE PAPER

BASEPLATE PAPER

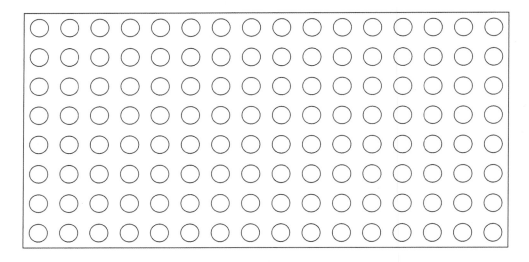

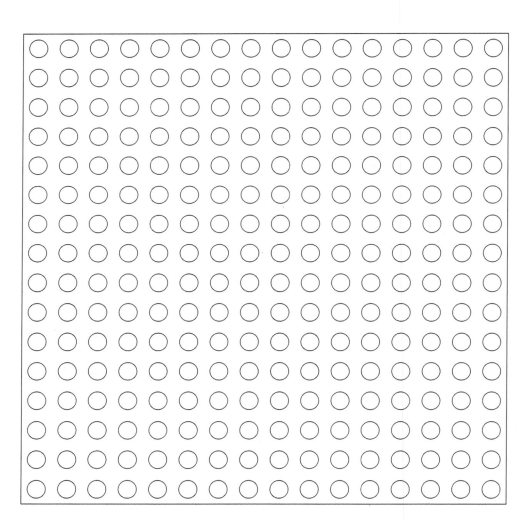

Made in the USA
Coppell, TX
19 November 2022